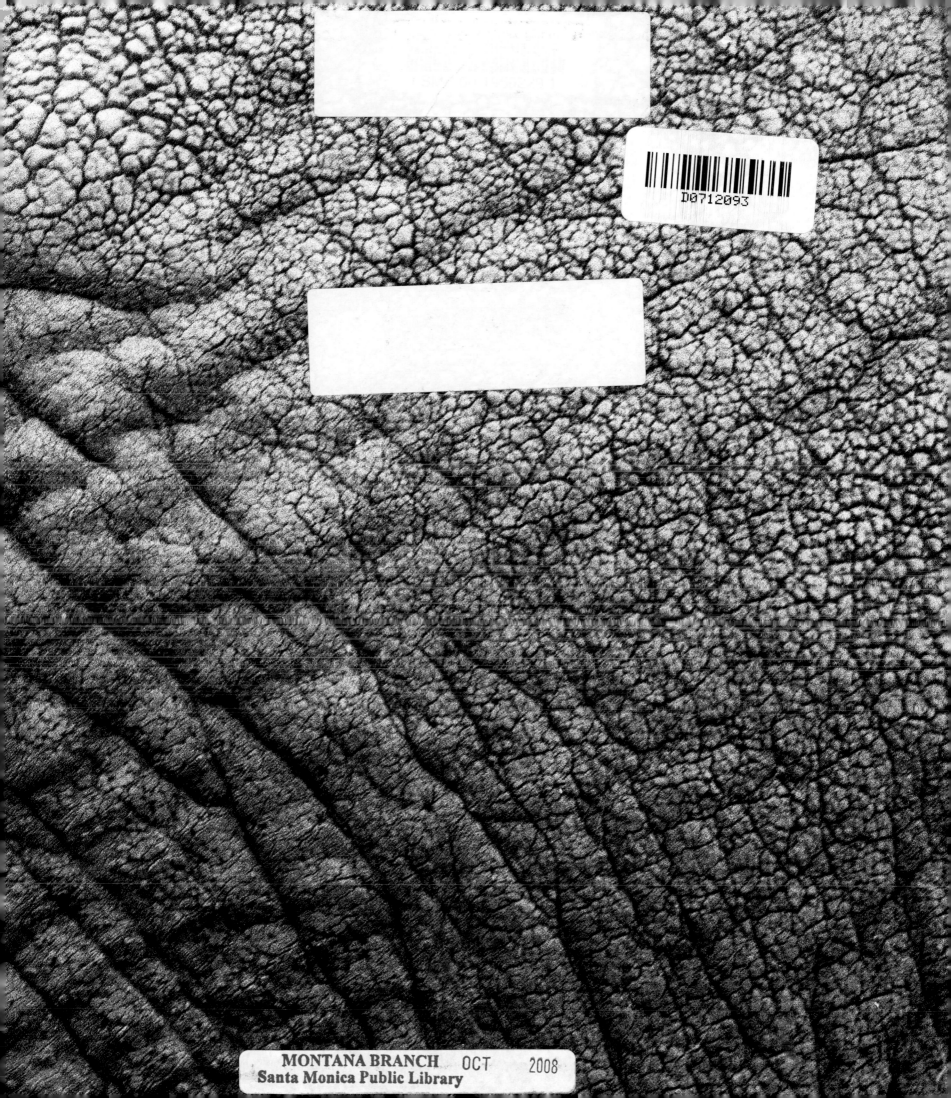

This book is dedicated to Timbo, who died in July, 2005.

The Elephant Book

yes the auriginal

THE ELEP

Nomi Baumgartl
Chris Gallucci

HANT MAN

Firefly Books

FOREWORD BY DANIEL OPITZ

"I love you" and "I could kill you." The world the Elephant Man grew up in was mean and hard. He left home when he was only twelve. Throughout his teens he was involved with the violent biker culture that developed in and around Los Angeles in the late sixties. Thanks to a falsified ID and too much pride to admit it, he found himself in jail for the first time at the tender age of seventeen.

His only true philosophy in those days was to show no weakness. While this mantra fueled the flames of his rebellion and brought him nothing but trouble, it also led to his eventual salvation: Timbo was a five-ton grey giant, who at nearly fifty years of age was North America's biggest and oldest African elephant bull. As stubborn as Chris himself, he too was unpredictable, fearless and always ready for a fight.

Chris was not looking for anything more than a job and perhaps some excitement when he rode his chopper into Acton, California, a small town on the edge of the Mojave Desert in 1975. He found a job as a welder on the insane set of the movie *Roar*, which starred over 100 wild lions, cougars, tigers and two elephants, as well as Hollywood diva and Hitchcock actress Tippi Hedren and her daughter Melanie Griffith.

When filming was completed, Chris and Tippi stayed behind with the wild animals. Together they converted what was left of the movie set into "Shambala — The Roar Foundation," a non-profit organization dedicated to providing the animals the best life possible. Chris, who was drawn to gigantic Timbo from the very start, asked if he could be the elephant's new trainer. He got the job.

To understand what it felt like to be an elephant, Chris spent the first night with Timbo, attaching himself to Timbo's chain and throwing away the key. To gain Timbo's trust, Chris learned to control his own demons. "See," he says, "The more relaxed and at ease I am, the more I allow Timbo to be free." In the nearly 30 years they spent together, neither Chris nor Timbo got into serious trouble again.

You do not come across people like Chris Gallucci simply by chance; you get caught in their gravitational field. Chris and I got to know each other in the Bahamas in 2000, during a photo shoot with Nomi Baumgartl. A model had invited him along for his first vacation in nearly 30 years. After just a few days, however, Chris cut his Caribbean trip short. He simply could not bear the thought that due to his absence, Timbo would be again be confined and chained. Chris returned to his own small world and self-imposed prison at Shambala.

I have always been drawn to people who have pushed the envelope throughout their lives, personalities who thrive on enormous challenge. A year later, when I arrived in Shambala with my film crew to document "The Elephant Man," Chris was in the midst of a huge personal crisis. For the first time he regretted his lonely life, confined to a ranch in the desert with Timbo. He shaved his long beard, sold his beloved chopper and stopped polishing his meticulously sharpened knives. But Chris would not be Chris if he did not manage to pull himself out of this deep depression. As filming progressed, he gradually found his balance again. He started his journal again, grew his beard back and bought a new motorcycle and a ´57 Chevy Bel Air that he had always wanted. We finished the film and became fast friends.

I valued Chris' simplicity, his attitude and way of looking at things, his entire essence, even Chris just being Chris. He never seemed to need such modern amenities as credit cards, computers or cell phones. Not because he was adverse to them, but because he was busy with other more important things. To me, he represented a sort of primal creature with an instinctive kind of wisdom and yes, an undertone of aggression. In a strange way, Chris became for me what Timbo was to him.

When photographer Nomi Baumgartl gets involved with a new subject it is not only with her camera, but also with her heart and entire being. Nomi was part of our film crew in Shambala. At one point she found herself in the middle of a fallow field with a five-ton elephant hurtling toward her. "Don't move!" Chris shouted, "Don't move!" Nomi closed her eyes and all was still. Suddenly she felt a moist, warm trunk in her face, and a suction so strong it felt as if she was being sucked into a wind tunnel. "Now he trusts you." At that moment she experienced the wondrous spiritual link between man and animal, Chris and Timbo.

"THAT'S THE DIFFERENCE BETWEEN
A HARLEY AND ANY OTHER BIKE...
I CAN MAKE THE LIONS ROAR."

"ONLY WHEN WE UNDERSTAND
WHAT DIVIDES US FROM THE
ANIMALS WILL WE BECOME
CLOSER TO EACH OTHER."

"ELEPHANTS.

DON'T MESS WITH THE ELEPHANTS."

"I AM TALKING ABOUT ELEPHANTS, MAN.
IT AIN'T EASY. BUT YOU DON'T HAVE TO BE
A ROCKET SCIENTIST TO FIGURE THEM OUT."

BLUE BOOK

ELIPHANTS

you wont forget

Name _____ GALLUCCI _____

Subject _____ Section _____

Instructor _____

Date _____ Seat No. _____

Ma tumbo Cora
5-13-79

②

My Life with Timbo

I live with an elephant — an elephant lives with me. I walk with an elephant — an elephant walks with me. I hang out with him — he hangs out with me. We relate and we understand each other ... so it's an understanding thing. I have the personality of an elephant and he has mine. It took 28 years to get to that point, now it's just become natural.

I never went to school. My parents were divorced and I left home when I was 12 years old and started living on my own. The first time I went to an adult jail I was only 16. I played the tough guy and I grew up fast, way too fast. I would always get in trouble; I kept getting arrested and kept getting into fights and kept getting busted all the time. It got me nowhere.

But that was the whole cool thing, man: be cool and you know, get a chopper and drive around America and raise as much hell as you possibly can and see how much trouble you can get away with. I've been shot, I've been stabbed, I've been beaten up and left for dead.

In those days there was only one way: show no weakness. That's it right there. That's the rules. That will get you through to the next day. I understand what it's like to be kicked when you're down. I understand what it's like to have your freedom taken away. I understand what it's like to be chained up. And maybe that's what got me the respect with the elephants: show no fear and show no weakness. If you can do that, you can survive in that world. If you can't — that world will eat you alive.

When I came here, me and my friend were just riding around, looking for jobs, and we rode into the town of Acton. It was just a little tiny town and we went to the bar there and got talking to the bartender. He said, "Yeah, up in the canyon they're filming a movie and they're hiring a lot of people." That's where *Roar* was being shot. The whole place had been built to film this movie and all the animals were here to do this movie. The big set house here behind me was here for the movie. The whole property was all about the movie.

When the mess was over I stayed behind and so did Tippi Hedren. I was living in a tent next to Timbo in the summertime. Then when winter came I stayed in a little tiny trailer and I hated the trailer. It was too small. So I built the living room and then decided, "I'm gonna live here!"

Tippi Hedren is the Hollywood actress — I'm the biker elephant trainer. Two totally different personalities, but I've gotten along with her so well because she lets me be me. She doesn't try to force her world on my world. Both of our worlds are on this ranch. Tippi understands how important the elephants are to me and I understand how important the ranch is to her. Somchow all that worked between us.

Friends, wives, family — I gave all that up to be with the elephant. I gave all that up. Hell, I've worked here for 28 years and I don't have a big retirement fund. I don't have anything. So it's not about money. It's about what happens to you when you get a connection to the biggest animal that walks the face of this earth. It got inside me. It didn't get inside my wallet. It got inside my heart and there's nothing I can do about it.

Maybe you'll understand how I get pulled apart between the things that I think I should do and my responsibility to the elephant if I tell you about one of the hardest things that ever happened to me. One day Timbo broke his tusk. He broke it real bad. He cracked it and he broke it way inside. That's bad when an elephant does that, because it can get infected back there and the infection can go to his brain and kill him. So you have to clean it. Three times a day you have to clean it out and dig out all the puss and then three times a day you have to pack it with medicine after removing the old stuff. Well, I get a phone call that my father had died and they were gonna have the funeral in two days and my sister is telling me, "You gotta come to the funeral," and I said, "I can't, I can't." The elephant would not let anyone else near him. So that is the problem that I have with life and with other people and with this elephant: I didn't even go to my own father's funeral. And am I a terrible person for doing that? But I know that I have to do this and I don't do the things that normal people do. I have to live with that.

Friends of mine tell me, "Chris, you've made your own prison. You've made your own jail in the way you've made your life. You have locked yourself in to these animals so much that you can't even get out of it in your mind." Oh my god, man, what a scary thought! I mean, I'm so into freedom and I'm so into not living by rules and regulations but now I find I've made my own rules and my own regulations. And now I've taken away my own freedom and I've done all this to myself, just because it was so important to give this elephant a good life.

When I'm with Timbo I don't think like a human. I'm not saying I become an elephant. I'm not saying that, but I get taken from one reality to another and I do prefer the reality with Timbo. Ours is a stubborn game. Who can be more stubborn? Like, he wants to keep turning that way and he knows I want to go this way.

Timbo has personality and I have personality. Sometimes people piss me off. Sometimes people piss him off, but I actually love that about him. Sometimes he can be a real son of a bitch. That's just so cool. His spirit has not been broken.

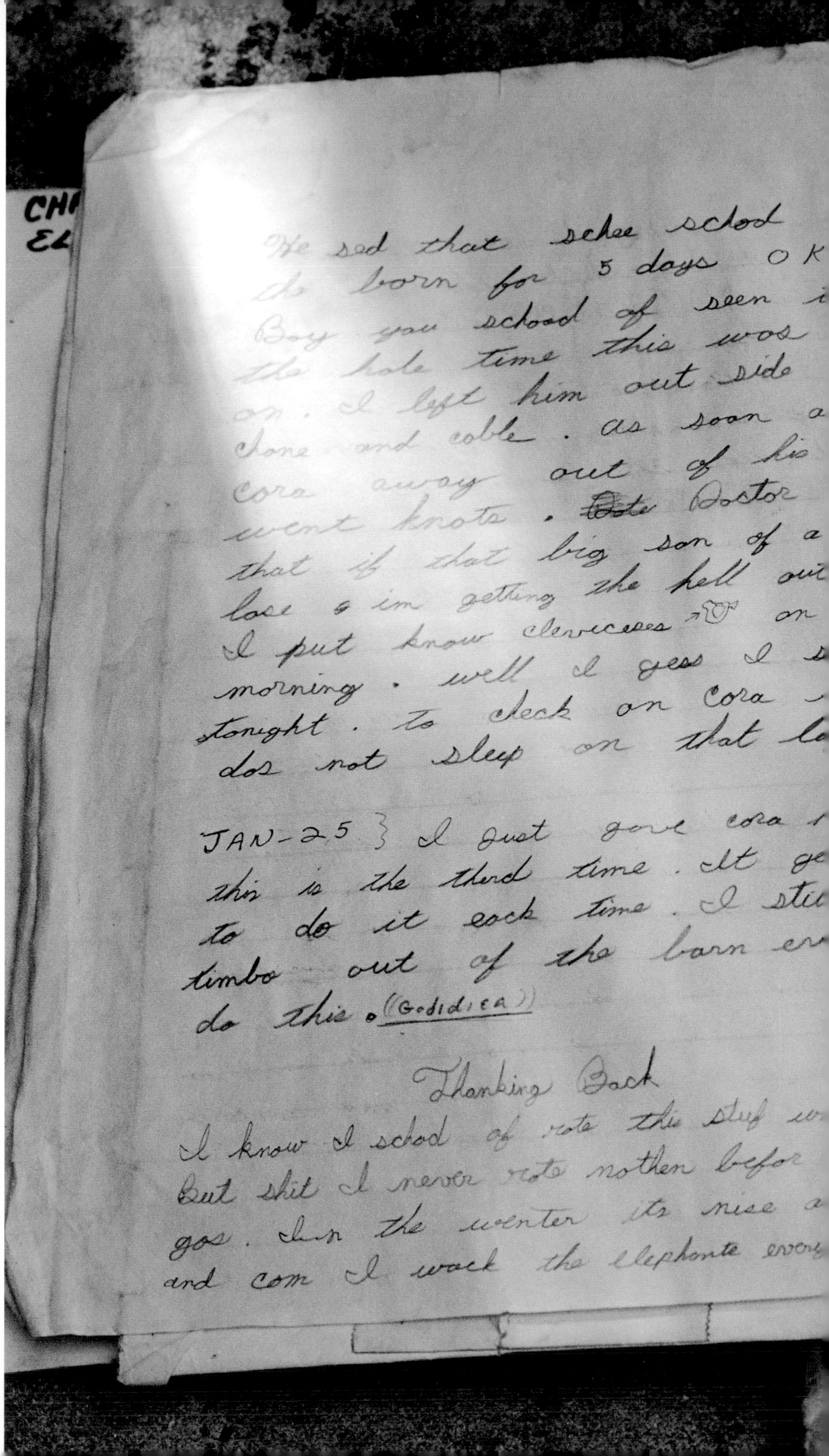

He sed that schee schod
do born for 5 days OK
Boy you schod of seen
the hole time this was
on. I left him out side
chane and coble. as soon a
cora away out of his
went knots. Bote Doctor
that if that big son of a
lose & im getting the hell ou
I put know clevicees ⚷ on
morning. well I gess I s
stonght. to cleck on cora
dos not sleep on that la

JAN-25 } I Just gove cora
this is the thrd time. It ge
to do it eock time. I sti
timbo out of the barn er
do this. (Godidica)

Thanking Back

I know I schod of rote this stuf
but shit I never rote nothen befor
gos. In the wenter its nise
and com I wock the elephante every

excepet wen it rains or its to cold. I hove them do thar trucks som times to keep them up on thar manners. But most the time I let them be them selves — ELEPHANTS ! dammet thots wate tha are. OH YES but the summer is greate. Its nise and hot in morrning so we go for a nise long walk. Then its the lake. I put them in the water I get in a connoe ~~~ and we have the time ~~~ of hour lives.

I did a T.V. show cald QUST once with the elephants in the water. and it worked out grate "OH SHIT" I rember once the hart to hart show asked me If I cod make a eliphant charge and destorey a tent. I sed sit sit hmmmm ("Shit Yes") But I diden't know how hard it is to get all that wate moveing in one direxicon amit twrde a taraget and tear it up. well every day I tray and tray. One week goes by and it ant so good oh he dose it but it dont look so good to me. Well more practis. O yes one week more and thot dam eliphant Timbo is rite on key. O yes after 4 tentes to wreake and a lot of crap. I even rented a motersycle to piss timbo off so he wood rinn full speed at his taraget. All of that and

14

15

Timbo is now 46 years old. He weighs five tons: 10,000 pounds. He's the oldest and largest African bull elephant in the Unites States. He may be a huge guy but we understand each other. I don't beat him. I'm not mean to him. I don't treat him bad, but I also don't leave him. I haven't left and I think that's the magic. That's when you get him to accept you in his life. He knows that I'm giving up my life for him.

Before this my life was — well, crazy, and the whole thing about never showing any fear, even if you're afraid — well, that's why things here fit me like a glove. It fits perfect, because when you have a problem you can't go, you know, "Oh god it's burning, and my god, the flood is rising and all I wanna do is run away." You have to just get into it. My background probably helped me to come to grips with my life here because I'm ready for anything. It doesn't matter what.

When Timbo starts blowing his horn and he gets angry and he starts running, I can't find someone else to jump in front of him and stop him. I will. I've always done it. It doesn't mean anything, except I'm just not afraid of him and he knows it. With somebody else, he will try and see how far he can push them, and if he knows he can keep pushing them, well he'll push them until they have no control of him. For years I have tried to find someone else to work with him, but I can't find anyone who is so dedicated they will stand in front of 10,000 pounds of pissed-off elephant.

I've talked to other elephant people and they all ask "How do you do this? How do you work with a bull all by yourself?" I always tell them the same thing. "I don't know how to do it any other way." I don't, you know, this is just the way I do it. I don't know really, honestly and truthfully what the "magic" is or what the "secret" is. I've read a lot of elephant books, I've watched a lot of people working with elephants and it didn't give me anything. I think the secret is dedication. That's the whole magic. That's the secret. You have to do it from your heart ... you have to really do it ... you can't just pretend to do it.

Timbo's answers are simple. That's what I like about him: it's not difficult and it's not complex. His answers are: I need food, I need water, I need exercise, I need to have fun — so help me do it. Naturally not all things are

that simple, but spending so much time to do the nothing, just hanging out with him, really makes me start thinking about what is important and what isn't important, and that gets really confusing. Because I'm getting older, you know. When I started doing this my beard was black and my hair was black and now my beard is grey and so is my hair. Is this all worth it? I don't know. So that pulls me apart inside, because sometimes I start thinking like, "Shit, did I blow it?" Because when he dies, he's the oldest elephant in the United States, and he's the largest African bull in the United States. I mean, I hope he doesn't die for a long time, but if he does ... I'm gonna be sitting here going, "What did I do? I spent 28 years with this huge feeling, with this huge emotion and now I have nothing."

All this insanity makes some kind of sense sometimes. Not too often, but it does when you show your kid snow for the first time, or when an elephant does the impossible and the unheard of for you, out of love and complete trust. Like when Timbo climbs straight up a small mountain because I asked him to. That kind of stuff makes you feel like you have done something kind of right with your life. I hope every person has some moments like these in their lives. Because I think these kind of moments make this crazy life all worth it, and I guess I am just a lucky guy.

When this is all over, I would like to teach people what I know. I think that would be a great ending to this whole story — or a great beginning to another story — to travel around and teach people who have elephants, teach them what I've learned about elephants over 28 years. I know a lot of things about what's going on with elephants when they get sick, and I know things just to keep them happy, things to keep them occupied, how to read their actions, how to tell when they're having problems. I know all of that. I have all of that in my mind. So I think that when this is all over, the thing to do would be to continue with this, but I wouldn't continue with him, because he'll be gone. So then I'll just continue with the elephant thing.

FROM CHRIS GALLUCCI'S JOURNAL
AND INTERVIEW WITH DANIEL OPITZ

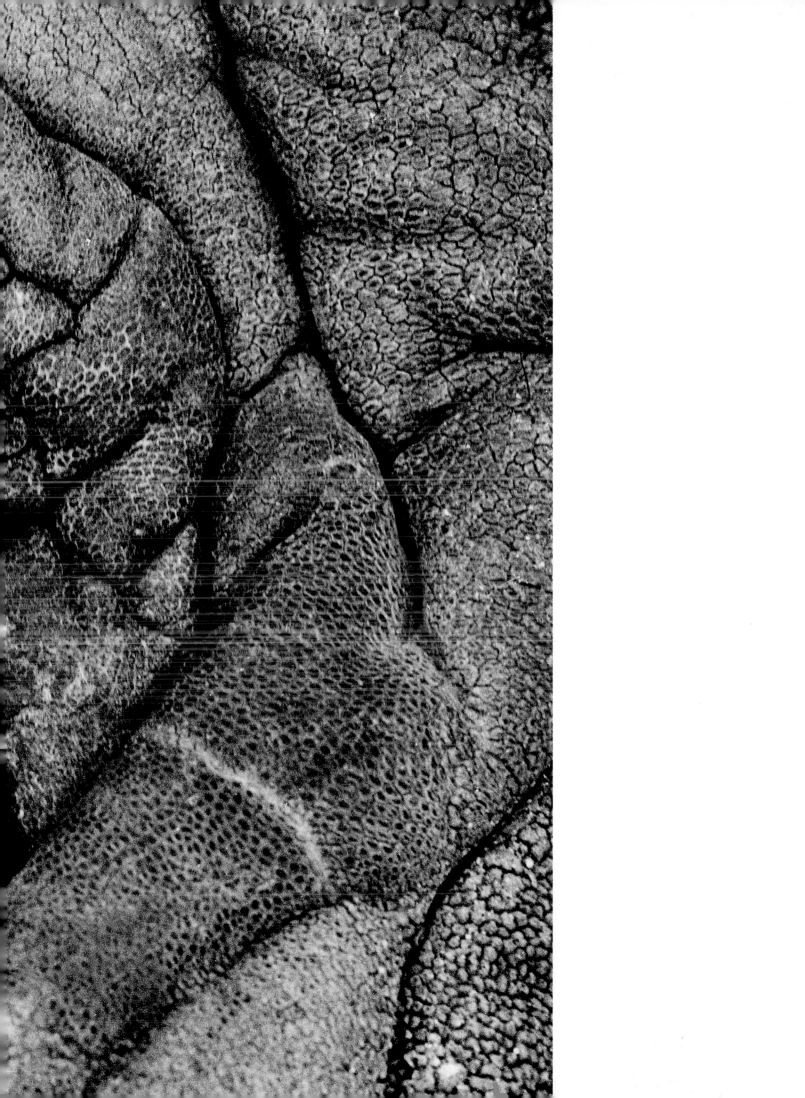

" ... FIVE TONS!"

"Oh, well, what can you expect when you start thinking and feeling like an elephant?"

"THE VET IS GETTING THE CREDIT,
THE OWNER IS GETTING THE CREDIT,
BUT THE TRAINER NEVER DOES.
THAT'S THE STORY OF MY LIFE."

"If you work them, you've got to love them,
figure them out, get inside their head,
get inside their heart and become one yourself.
They will come to know you the same way."

"WHAT THE HELL IS GOING ON?"

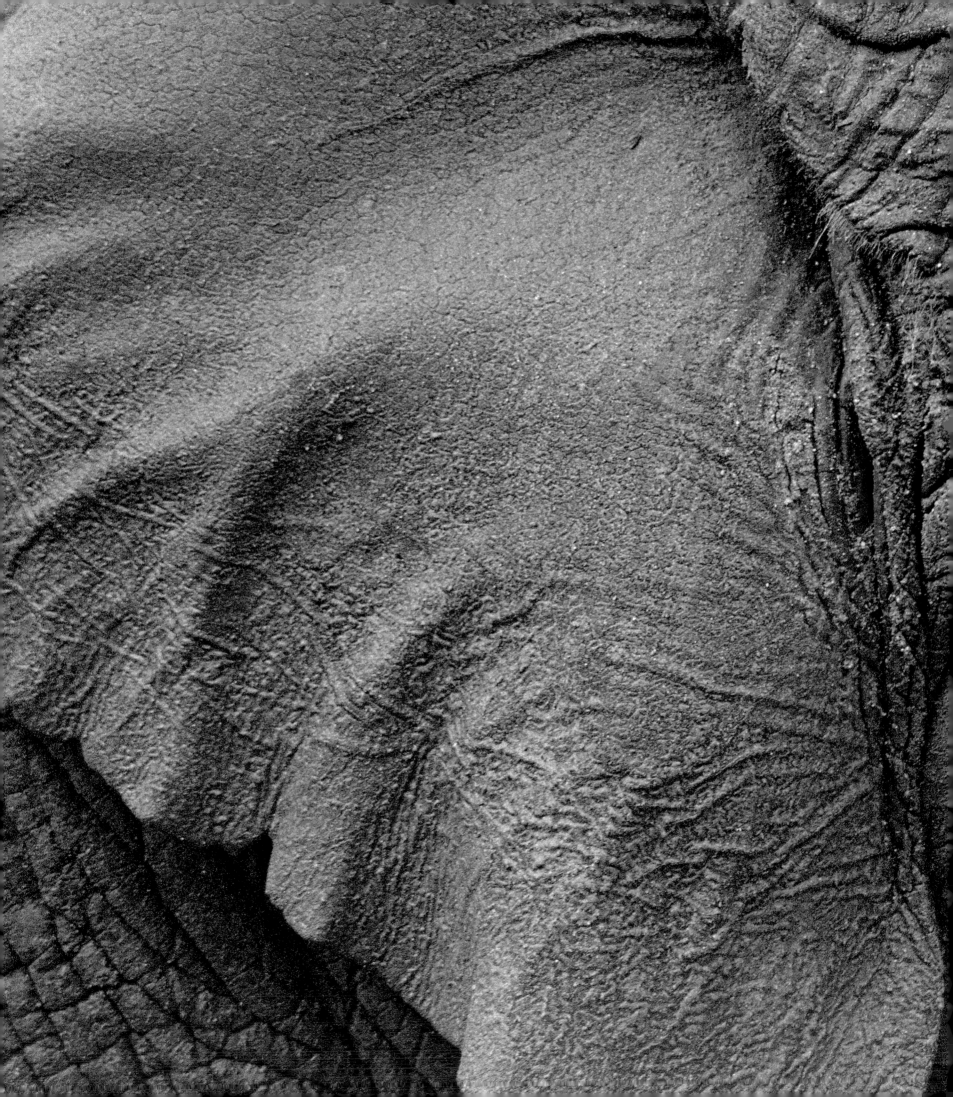

"THEY FEEL PAIN. THEY HAVE FEELINGS.
AND YES, HAPPINESS. FULFILLMENT, FREEDOM AND FRIENDSHIP."

"I'VE GOT TO DO THE ELEPHANT'S FEET TOMORROW.
TOENAILS. IT AIN'T SO BAD
          IF YOU'VE GOT A SHARP FILE."

SHIT I DON'T
NO THE DATE
NOV ? 91

REAMIND ME TO TELL YOU ABOUT
BEVRLEY HIL'S 3 FUCHEN LOYOURS
A SQUNFINER AND TIPPI. FOR A
ELEPHANT DEPSIT. SO TODAY
WE HADE A FUND RASER A LOT
OF PEPLE. ENEYWAY AT THE
END TIPPI WAS TACKEN
TO A CROUD. I WASE DONE DOING
ELEPHANT PITCHERS. SO I TOLD
TIPPI I WASE GOING TO LODE THE
BARN. I WONTED TO SE IF TIPPI
WOOD CONTU HERE SPECH IF I
WOSENT THAR. SO I SOLWLE WALKED
AWAY AND YES HE DID IT THRU
ROCKS AT THE PEPLE. SO THIS
IS CAL TECHING TIPPI TRICKS.
AND ALL IT IS IS KEPPING THE
ELEPHANTS ATTCHEN. AND YOUR
EYE ON HIM OR HER. NOT SO SCHEE
CAN STAND THAR AND GIV SPECHESS WHEN
I ANT THAR. BUT SO SCHEE CAN
AT LEST WALK BY AND OR JUST
SAY HI. WITHOUT PLAYING CATCH
WITH A ELEPHANT

THE ONE HILL OF
YOU BEN LOOKING

"I don't know the date.
That is one of the things
I like about my life."

"PLEASE DON'T LET ME BE MISUNDERSTOOD."

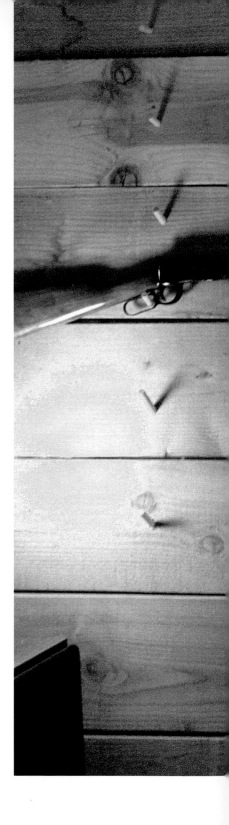

"WHEN I WAS A KID, I WANTED TO
BE A GANGSTER. SO I GREW UP FAST
... TOO FAST THE FIRST TIME I
GOT ARRESTED I WAS IN THE SIXTH
GRADE, AND I WAS TOO STONED TO
SPELL MY NAME. AS TIME WENT ON
THINGS DIDN'T GET ANY BETTER."

"STOP THE PROBLEM

BEFORE IT HAPPENS."

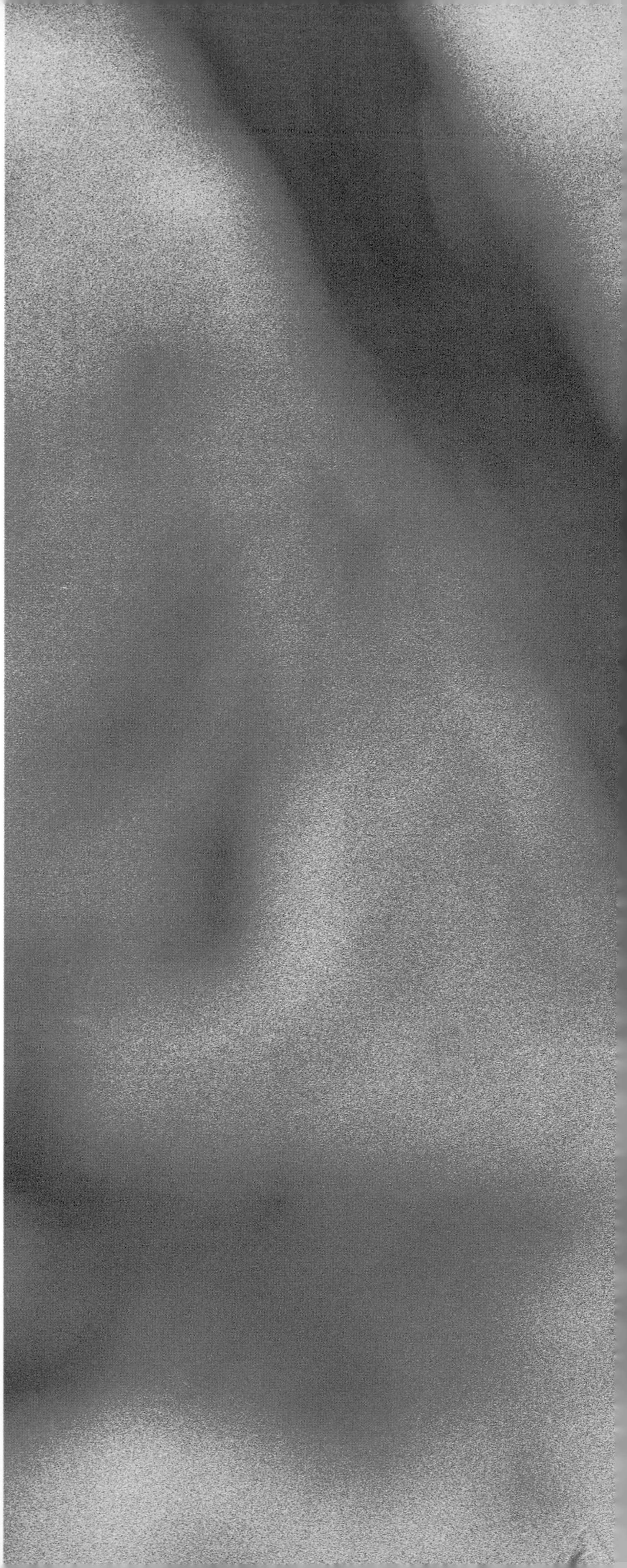

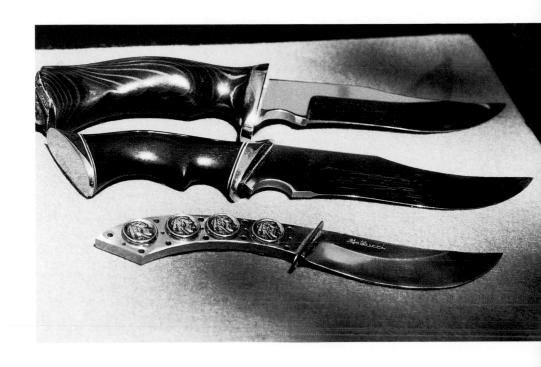

"I SPEND A LOT OF TIME JUST POLISHING THINGS.
I POLISH MY BIKE, I POLISH MY KNIVES. I MEAN,
I SPEND SO MUCH TIME DOING IT, BUT THE MORE
TIME I SPEND, THE MORE TIME THE ELEPHANT
GETS TO STAY OUT."

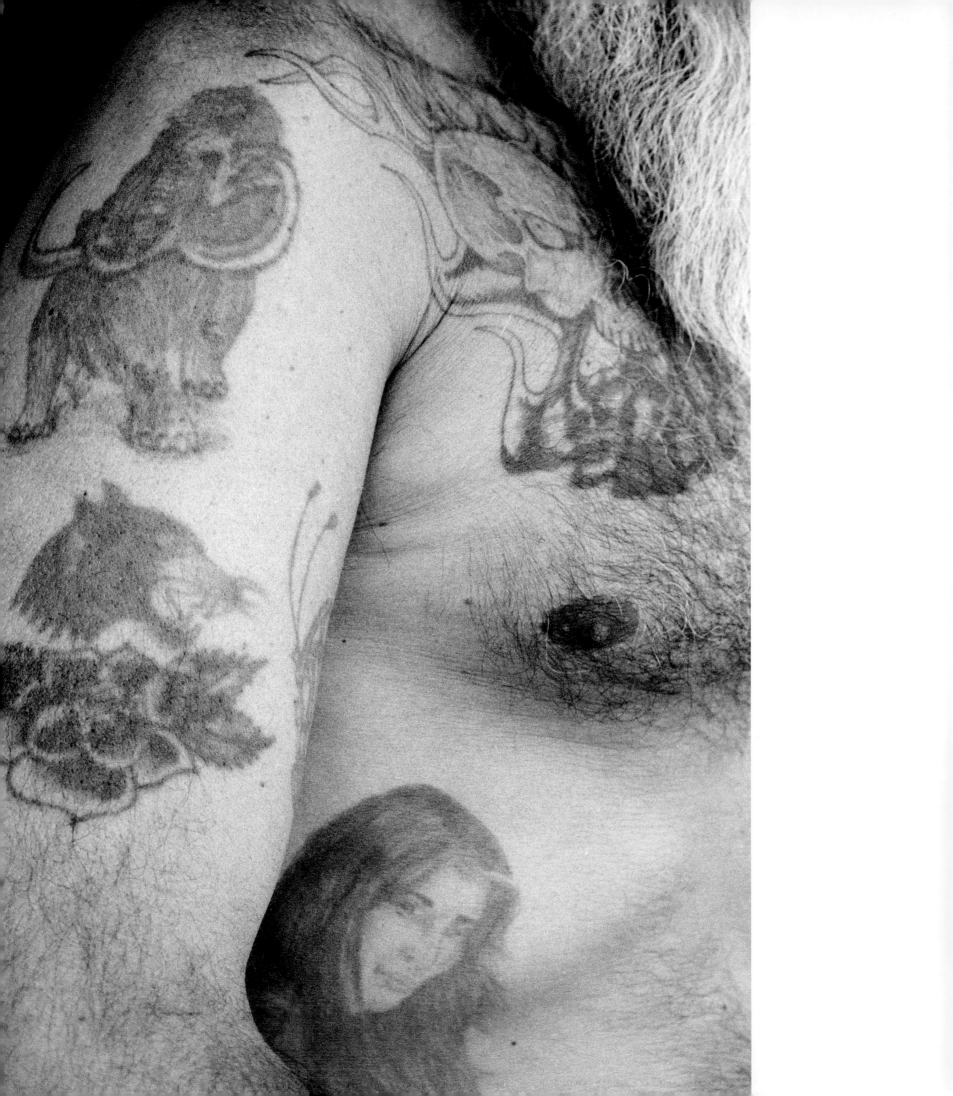

"THAT'S JUST HOW I AM."

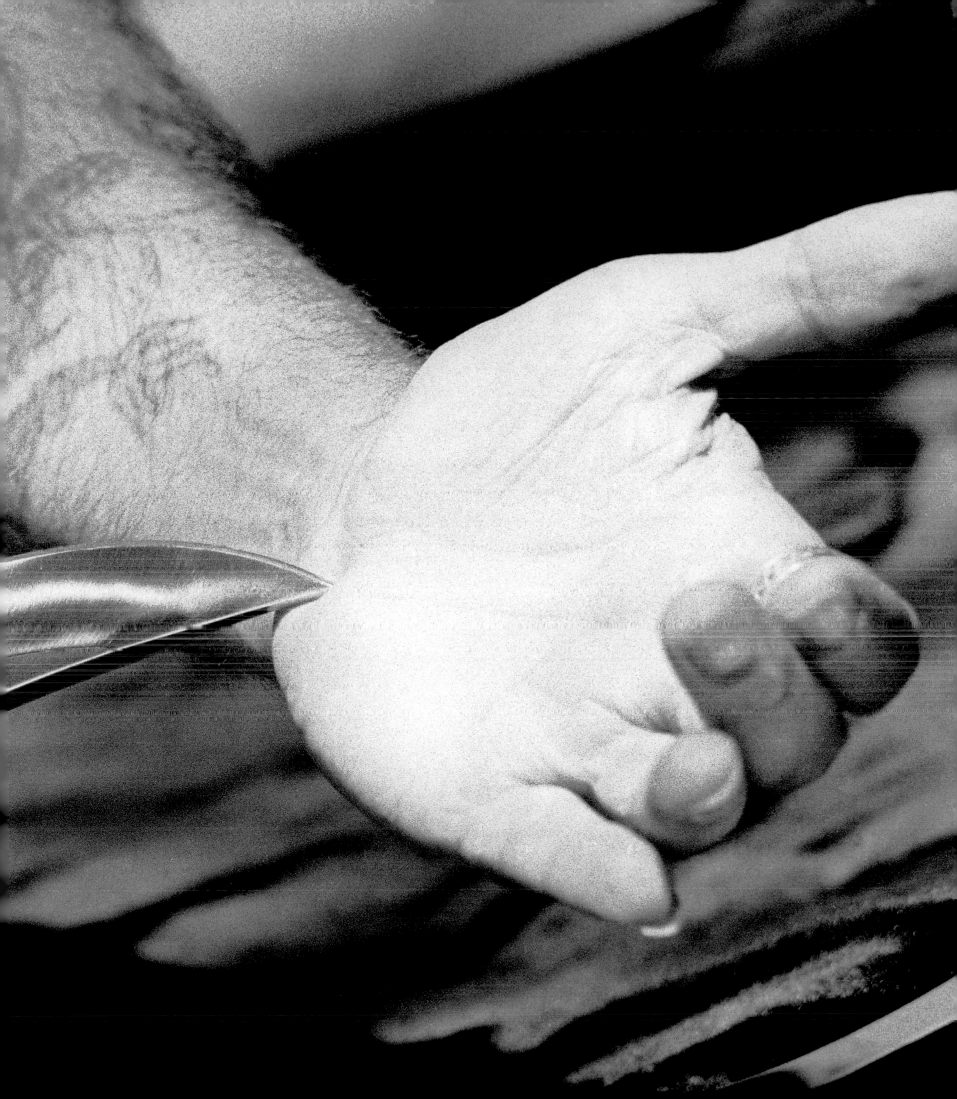

"It has to be a Harley, and it has to be a chopped Harley."

"It's the whole feeling. It's the sound.
It's, it's — it's a way of life, you know.
I can't ride something else.
I wouldn't ride something else."

"You have to live for something or someone, otherwise life doesn't make much sense."

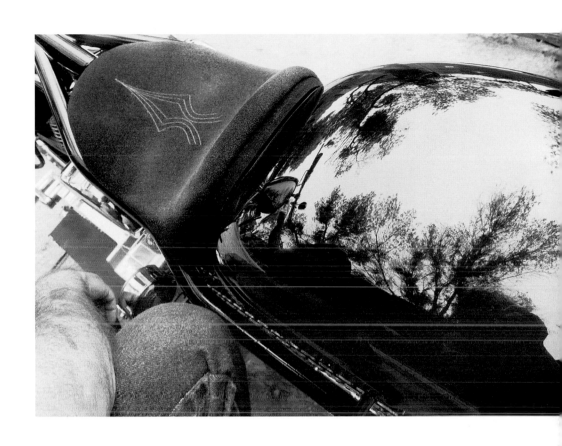

"IT'S INSANE.

    IT'S INSANITY IN BLACK AND CHROME."

"I UNDERSTAND WHAT IT'S LIKE
TO BE CHAINED UP."

"Out here I follow him. He doesn't follow me ... until we go back. When we come out here, I just follow him, so he gets to do whatever he wants to do. So we trade roles. We switch places. So here I get to study him and see what he does, how he does it, and I learn so much about him."

"If he is in the yard, then I try to make the yard as nice as I can for him. So this is all natural, stuff he would get in the riverbed. Yeah, he likes it. So then he'll sit in the yard and he'll eat all of this and he'll take all of the bark off the branches, and it's all healthy for him. I just treat him like I want to be treated. I want my food to look good so I make his food look good."

"No, I have not lost my mind. But that elephant told me that he was sick of drinking the fucking old lake water. He didn't tell me in words, but it was very clear. So I started giving him fresh well water to drink."

"YOU KNOW, SOMETIMES I SIT AND THINK THAT THERE IS A WHOLE WORLD OUT THERE, A LOT TO SEE AND A WHOLE LOT OF DIFFERENT THINGS TO DO. BUT THAT IS ONLY SOMETIMES, BECAUSE I WOULD NOT TRADE MY LIFE WITH ANYBODY."

"I LIKE THE MEDIEVAL, YOU KNOW —

OLD TIME, WARRIOR STUFF.

SO I HAVE A LOT OF IT AROUND ME.

I SORT OF SURROUND MYSELF IN THINGS THAT I LIKE.

THEN WHEN I WAKE UP IN THE MORNING,

I WAKE UP IN AN ENVIRONMENT THAT I CHOSE."

"I LOOKED OVER AND NOTICED THESE PEOPLE WERE STARING AT ME, SO I GO, "WHAT ARE YOU GUYS STARING AT?" AND THEY SAY, "YOU LOOK SO OUT OF PLACE WHEN YOU'RE NOT AT THE RANCH." AND WHENEVER I GO PLACES, PEOPLE SAY "WOW, WHAT ARE YOU DOING HERE?"

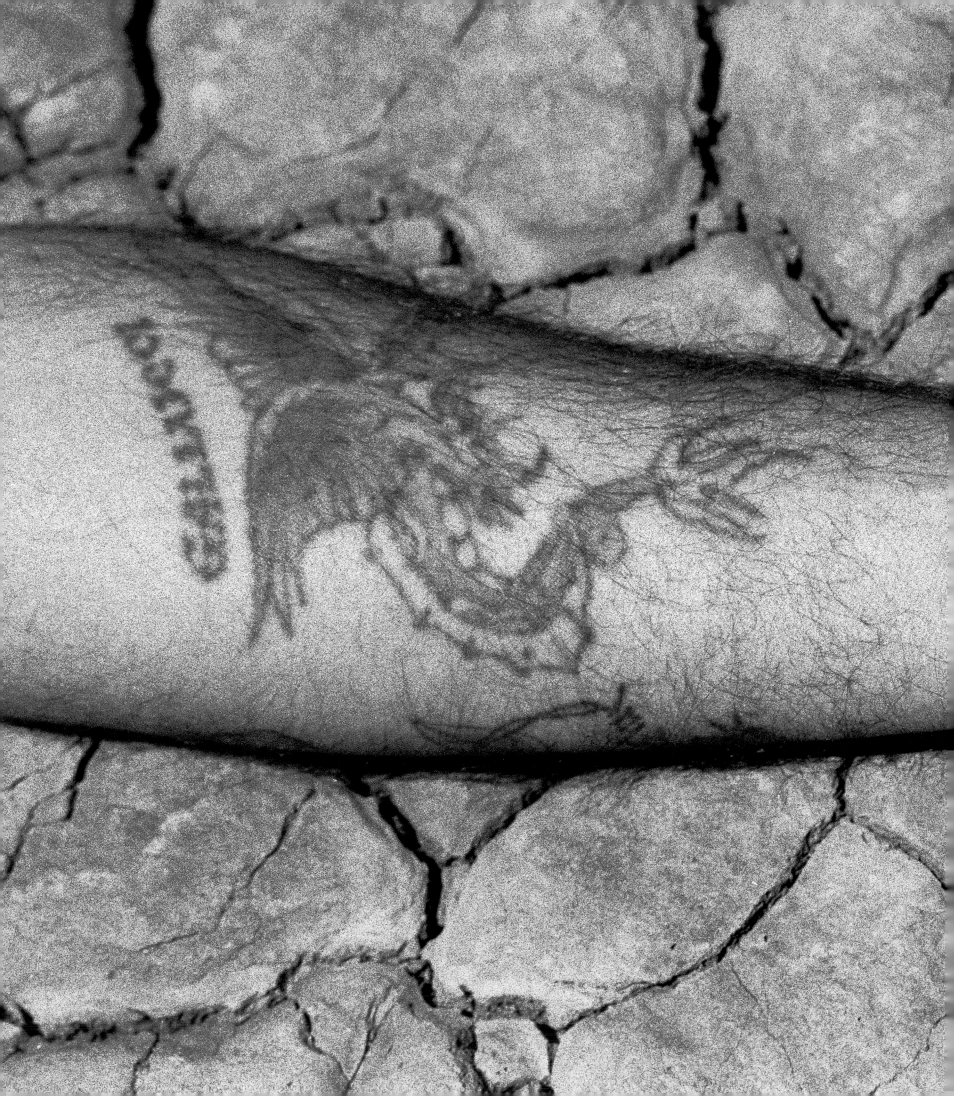

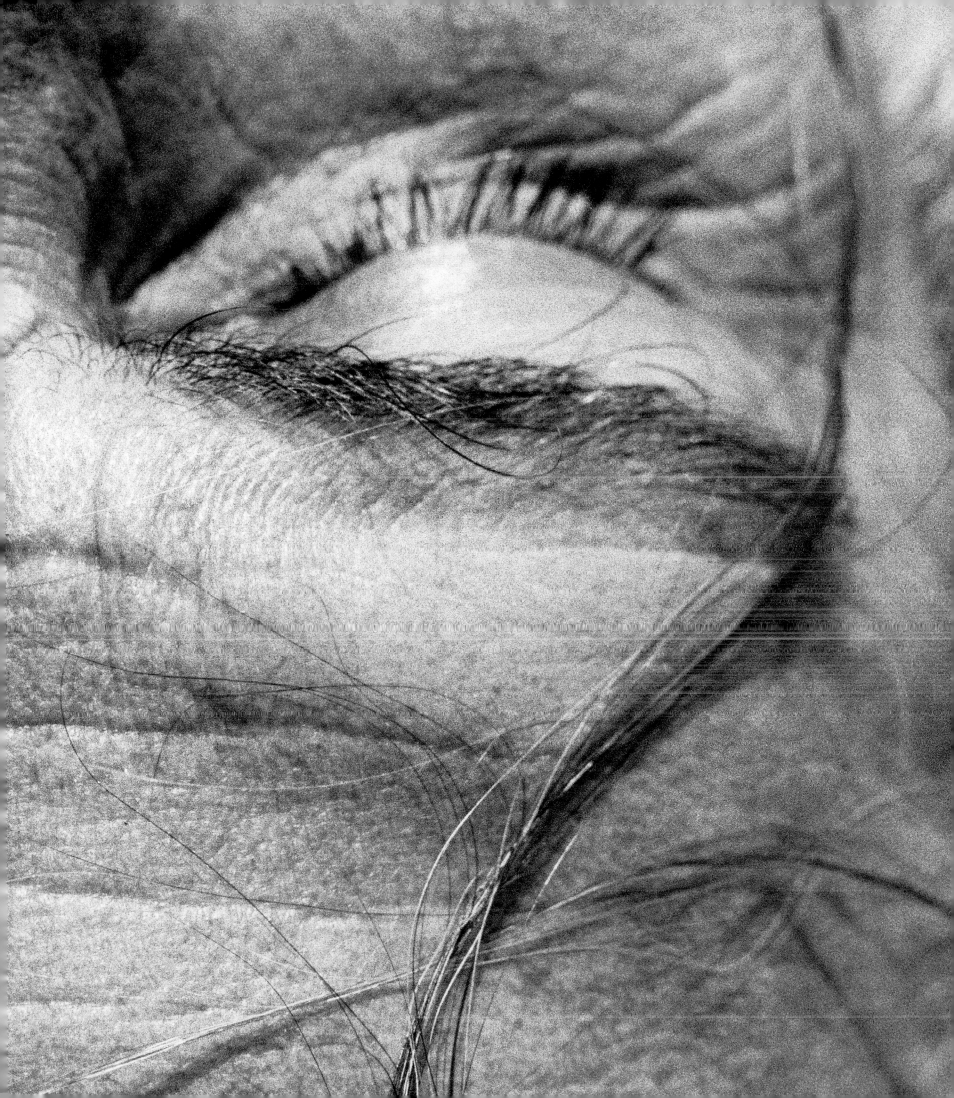

"You can't shake it, it's a good thing,
but it will cost, and I ain't talking money.
I am talking wives, friends, time to do the nothing."

"Sometimes I look around me and all my stuff and think that I did not fuck up. I came up with something."

Thoughts after Timbo Died

How did I feel after Timbo's death? Empty. It was amazing. It was incredible. It was horrible. I mean when your best friend dies in your arms, basically. And my best friend happened to be an elephant.

When Timbo died I didn't have anybody, but I would rather it's me being left alone than him being left alone. So it's real, real, difficult to deal with, but he gave me so much for 30 years, and that overpowers the sadness.

After he died I went away and just left the ranch. I got on my motorcycle and rode around for hours and hours. I would find a place and sit down and think, and that was real lonely. It was real. This is what it feels like not having an elephant.

However, he's still with me. He's always with me. I feel him inside. It'll get colder or there is something to do and I'll look at the other guys that work with me and tell them, "Look, we got to — " and then I'll go, "Never mind." I'm getting ready to say "Now we gotta load the barn, we gotta get him in before he gets too cold." I think that it's life replaying in my brain, which is a good thing.

There are so many memories. I mean, this whole place is memory. The barn you know, there was an elephant in it for so long and now it's empty. It's like history. That's how history is made. When you look back in time and you look at history itself, most people who made history are gone, but as long as you still remember them and still speak their names, they are still with you and you feel them. So mine just happened to be an elephant. I don't want to let it go. I'll never lose these memories and so in my mind he still lives. Who knows, man, if there's an elephant heaven then he's probably running around with a bunch of other elephants.

I don't know. He's here in spirit and I am happy about that.

Timbo got sick that night and we tried to save him. It lasted all day and all night. I was so exhausted that I just went home and went to bed, and then when I got up it was hard to believe. It was like a dream. I sat there by myself and didn't want to talk to anybody and I didn't want to go anywhere, and then I could feel his energy, his power. I don't know if it was just memories coming alive or what it was. I could feel it inside me, and then it started getting bigger and bigger and almost painful, and I'm sitting there thinking, "Oh my god, this elephant is coming into me in some way." I could feel him, and he was too big to come inside me. I'm just a human being, and to feel 10,000 pounds of elephant inside me just set me back down. I would get up and walk across the room and think "What's happening?" and I would sit and just start thinking about him. Whenever he came back inside me whatever which way, his spirit was too big for my body. It was a transition. It took weeks. That's why I couldn't come back to the ranch. I had to let it happen, whatever it was. It was such a huge emotional thing, and it was the biggest emotional thing I've ever had to deal with. It was an emotional thing as big as Timbo. It was almost too big.

I can close my eyes. I can see him, but that happens to everybody who loses something close to them. But what I experienced was much bigger than anything I could ever imagine. Maybe it's because he was the largest animal that walks the face of the earth, and I had such a close and tight relationship with him, and I was with him when he died. It would have been twice as horrible if I wasn't here, if I wasn't

here to help him die. He wanted it you know, he was getting sick. His body was shutting down. He was ready to go. It would have been real selfish not to let him go. So it was to honor his soul and his spirit that I let him go with dignity. I will remember him as long as I live.

When I talk to people, they always ask me about the last days. Usually they want to know about his illness. I don't go there. I mean, I lived it. I go for long walks in the field. That was one of my most favorite things with him. Walks in the riverbed, sitting in my house and hearing him blow his horn, him playing in the water and throwing tires around. That's the stuff I remember and that's the stuff that went on for 30 years.

The last year was the death year. He was deteriorating in his mind, he was going and he took a while to go. That was the devastating part. I like to remember the good part of it. I prefer to go to the happy places where we had great times. The long walks with Timbo. I'd make a left turn, he'd make a left turn. I wouldn't even have to tell him. I'd go right, he'd go right and so it wasn't difficult. It was a huge bonding between man and animal that we created ourselves. We were simply two living beings, a human and an animal, two living spirits that came together and understood each other and liked each other. And when I sit back and think of him, that's what I think of.

I don't know much about spirituality and other things that go on in the world but I do know me and I know my life and I know what I feel, and I can feel him. When I enter his space in the barn I can really feel him. But the cool thing is, he goes with me when I leave his space, and that's such a nice thing to have with you and I don't want to let it go. It's memories of my best friend. Thirty years of them. That's a lot of memories. That's a long relationship and I just happen to be the guy whose best friend was an elephant.

When the trees start getting green and flowers start blooming, I think: "Hmmm, boy, he'd like that." But now he is not here, you know. When the grass starts getting really luscious green and it starts growing then we'd always cut it for him. So I walk through the grass and think, "God, he'd love this."

I think it's a good thing not to pretend that you don't have any feelings. You don't let these feelings go through you like the wind through a chain link fence. Forget it that men stand there like a wall and let the wind bounce off them and then it really

tries to knock them over. I feel Timbo everywhere. I feel him in the shower. I feel him on my motorcycle. I feel him in my car. I feel him when I'm in an airplane. And that's a nice thing, because he goes with me and he never could before. So now he does.

See, some people think about Timbo and get sad. I think about him and get happy. So I don't think about the last day and I think you are cheating yourself if you do that. If all the people in the world who've ever lost their best friend or someone close to them, if they sit there and just think about the last days, they're cheating themselves. That's not what their life was all about. They had good days and good times, so you shouldn't just think about the last days. When you ask me to think about my elephant, instead of a sad, miserable look I get a smile, because that elephant was wonderful. He was the most amazing animal and the whole relationship was so amazing. Sure, it's a drag to be an elephant man without an elephant. It's like a soldier without a uniform. People look at me differently and I really don't care. What I do care about is what's inside me and what he gave me, and that I am grateful for.

FROM CHRIS GALLUCCI'S JOURNAL
AND INTERVIEW WITH DANIEL OPITZ

"LIFE IS LIKE A PLACE YOU'VE NEVER BEEN BEFORE.
AS SOON AS YOU FIGURE IT OUT, IT'S TIME TO GO."

caled a docter Beaman she sed that
it mite be a ....
explode it ....
sed that it didnt ......
be fair. he sed to ....
towels on the bump and ....
I starte ------ to ....
HOT TOWELS ~~evrey~~ hour so .....
started • every hour
long July 1 tuesday the ....
~~TMENT~~ all day timbo ....
.... the TOWELS at all
July 2 the same ....
.... doun or ....
tembre dasent ....
~~un~~comfortable at all. ... that
lunp didnt look so good at first
JULY 3 Still with the hot towels
but not evrey hour AT LEAST
not all night long and the lunp

④   ⑪

WARNING
ELEPHANTS ARE EXTREMELY
DANGEROUS - NO LOITERING
KEEP OUT

"I was once the

keeper of the beast."

"Fried,

fizzled

and fucked."

"I USED TO OPEN MY EYES
AND SEE ELEPHANTS. NOW
I ONLY SEE THEM WHEN
MY EYES ARE CLOSED."

Back to the roots
Epilog by Nomi Baumgartl

My journey to the Okavango Delta was a symbolic trip, a search for evidence. I needed to go back to Africa, the cradle of both humankind and the biggest mammals on this earth: the African elephants. I wanted to go back to Timbo's roots.

As I watched the silhouette of the small plane below me, I surrendered to the dreams I had when Timbo first came close to me – enduring and intense dreams. Possibly the image of the plane's shadow can be used as an allegory for dreams becoming reality. I wanted to capture these dreams with my camera and externalize them as traces of light from an imaginary journey of three beings. Because in my imagination I was not traveling alone. Timbo and Chris Gallucci, the Elephant Man, were with me. I made them a gift of the wonderful impressions seen through my eyes.

Chris's great dream to free his elephant, to allow him to escape back into the wild, goes back more than 10 years. At that time, he contacted Randall J. Moore, who had established a re-introduction program for African elephants from the American circus and film world. However, Moore's answer was somewhat disheartening: "Timbo is already too old, even if he went into the program with Chris." In the meantime, Timbo has passed away and claimed another kind of freedom.

What a sense of joy it would give me now to give the Elephant Man the African wilderness, the elephant heaven on earth. This was the reason for me to go back, back to the roots: to trace his philosophy and follow it, and pass it on.

Kane the bushman was my guide. His excellent tracking skills and close communication with nature and the wild enabled us to track down the elephants. When we found the first elephant herd, it was a touching encounter, full of curiosity on both sides. What a moving moment! This is how Timbo's life could have been.

I was only made aware of the real size of these earthly mammoths when I saw the skull of an elephant bull. I just let the image sink in. It felt for a moment as if it grew bigger and bigger, as big as a monument, alive again with a spirit and a soul. Kane was celebrating a ritual, which I captured on film as a memorial to Timbo.

When leaving, I found a fragment of ivory. It was the most beautiful present that Africa could have given me. I took it to an ebony tree whose silhouette rose in the sky and seemed to guard the elephant herd from above. The elephants had lovingly left traces in the bark. I found a place in the trunk where elements of nature, ebony and ivory had united together in perfect harmony.

To be one means the yearning for unity, as in the lives of Chris and Timbo. Back to the roots means securing roots for the future and the hope that the Elephant Man can look on life in a different way without Timbo. The hope that he will find a vision of the future written in the tracks of his departed elephant friend.

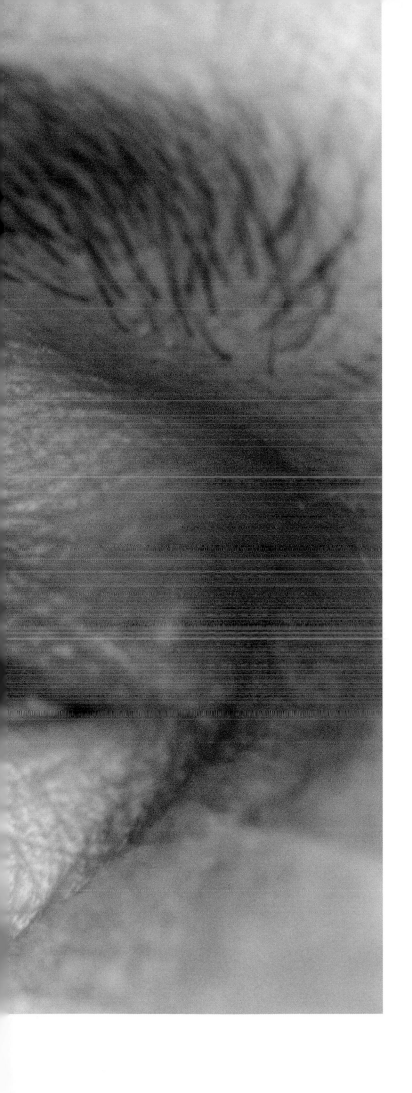

"If there's an elephant heaven,
then he's running around
with a bunch of other
elephants."

NOMI BAUMGARTL is an internationally-
acclaimed photographer who lives in Munich and all
over the world when required by her projects. Her life's
work lies in showing in pictures the connection between
man and nature, and between the sea and the land, as a
tribute to creation. Nomi Baumgartl's work has received
prestigious awards and her pictures are frequently
published and exhibited. This professional photographer
is now also an author. Timbo's story served as
inspiration for her book Muno, a poetic tale about an
elephant that straddles dream and reality. She is a
member of the Bilderberg Photography Agency and an
envoy for dolphin aid.
www.I-WONDER-NOMI.com

CHRIS GALLUCCI is an author, biker and elephant trainer who lives in Acton, California. His youth was alternately spent on the streets and in jail. He devoted the past 30 years of his life to Timbo, the biggest and most dangerous African elephant in North America. What began as a violent and angry life turned into a tender friendship between two stubborn creatures. Although Chris can barely write, he kept a detailed diary during his three decades as an elephant trainer. Since Timbo's death, Chris has continued to work as Preserve Supervisor at "Shambala," the wild animal preserve on the edge of the Mojave Desert. www.shambala.org

DANIEL OPITZ is an author and filmmaker, and heads the production company Ocean Mind, with offices in Kiel, Germany, and Maui, Hawaii. His film projects have focused on the emotional and spiritual conflict between man and nature. In 2000 he produced his seminal work Ka Nalu Nui, a documentary about the greatest wave in the world. The Elephant Man followed in 2003, a film about the friendship between biker Chris Gallucci and the elephant bull Timbo. Both films have been widely shown on television and have won awards at numerous film festivals. Currently, Daniel Opitz is working on Whales in Mind, a movie and TV production about the unique relationship between whales and people. You can find more information and DVDs about this project on www.ocean-mind.com.

ACKNOWLEDGEMENTS

NOMI BAUMGARTL: I thank …

TATJANA PATITZ for her introduction to the Elephant Man.

DIRK WALBRECKER, who pointed the publishers to the elephant trail and shared it with great enthusiasm.

CONTANZE WILD for her many discussions that helped focus the elephant theme; and for her help in Africa during the photo shoot of "Back to the Roots."

LEICA CAMERA AG, especially Steffen Keil.

WILDERNESS SAFARIS for their generous support in the Savuti and Abu camps in Botswana. This undertaking exemplifies wilderness conservation efforts.

KANE, the bushman, for his "wilderness education."

RANDALL J. MOORE and his team in Camp Abu in Botswana, especially DR. SYBILLE QUANDT, who as large animal veterinarian developed the elephant wilderness program and led the international elephant protection effort.

ANKE DEGENHARDT, Director of Photography at Park Avenue.

JORGE SCHMIDT, whose knowledge and competence managed to bring all elements of this book together.

ARNO DREXLER, who magically readied my photographs for publication, so that this work would see the light of day.

IRIS FOSTER, whose keen eye and competent editing brought pictures and text together.

TIMBO AND CHRIS, who entrusted me with their confidence and showed me the deep link between the human and elephant spirits.

… and all others who are not named individually here for their assistance in bringing this work to fruition, and especially to publishers MONIKA THALER and GERT FREDERKING.

DANIEL OPITZ: I thank …

TIPPI HEDREN, for enlivening our film set with her Hollywood charisma, endless charm and timeless beauty.

NDR Naturfilm and MSH for their steady confidence in me and my project.

STEPHAN REINSCH, FLORIAN MELZER and IDA VON SALZWEDEL for their steady support in all the important life and production phases.

A FIREFLY BOOK

Published by Firefly Books Ltd. 2008

English translation © 2008 Firefly Books

Originally published as Der Elefantenmann
Copyright © 2007 Frederking & Thaler GmbH, Munich

First printing

Published in the United States by
Firefly Books (U.S.) Inc.
P.O. Box 1338, Ellicott Station
Buffalo, New York 14205

Published in Canada by
Firefly Books Ltd.
66 Leek Crescent
Richmond Hill, Ontario L4B 1H1

Photographs: Nomi Baumgartl, Munich
Author photos (Nomi Baumgartl/Daniel Opitz): Constanze
   Wild, Diessen am Ammersee
Text: Chris Gallucci, Acton, California
Foreword and interviews:
   Daniel Opitz, OCEAN MIND, Kiel and Maui, Hawaii
Pages 26–37 and 116–127:
   Journal sketches by Chris Gallucci and quotes from Daniel
   Opitz on the filming of The Elephant Man, OCEAN MIND
Epilog: Nomi Baumgartl, Munich

Book design: BURO JORGE SCHMIDT, Munich
English translation: Klaus Brasch

Publisher Cataloging-in-Publication Data (U.S.)

Gallucci, Chris.
    Elephant man / Chris Gallucci, Nomi Baumgartl ; with
introduction by Daniel Opitz.

Originally published as: Der Elefantenmann / Chris
Gallucci; Munich: Frederking & Thaler Verlag Gmbh, 2007.
[160] p.: photos. (some col.); cm.
Summary: Powerful photographs document the intense,
thirty-year relationship between Chris Gallucci, biker and
ex-con, and Timbo, the largest bull elephant in North
America.

ISBN-13: 978-1-55407-422-8
ISBN-10: 1-55407-422-3

1. Gallucci, Chris — Personal narratives. 2. Timbo
(Elephant). 3. Elephants — Legends and stories. 4.
Elephants — Training. I. Baumgartl, Nomi. II. Opitz,
Daniel. III. Title.
599.61096/092 [B] dc22   QL737.P98.G3G3 2008

Library and Archives Canada Cataloguing in Publication

Gallucci, Chris
    The elephant man / Chris Galluci, Nomi Baumgartl.

ISBN-13: 978-1-55407-422-8
ISBN-10: 1-55407-422-3

1. Gallucci, Chris. 2. Elephants—Biography.
3. Human-animal relationships. 4. Elephant trainers—
United States—Biography.
I. Baumgartl, Nomi, 1950- II. Title.

QL737.P98G34 2008   636.9'676092   C2008-902659-4

Printed in China

"OF ALL FOOTPRINTS, THOSE OF THE ELEPHANT ARE SUPREME."

BUDDHA

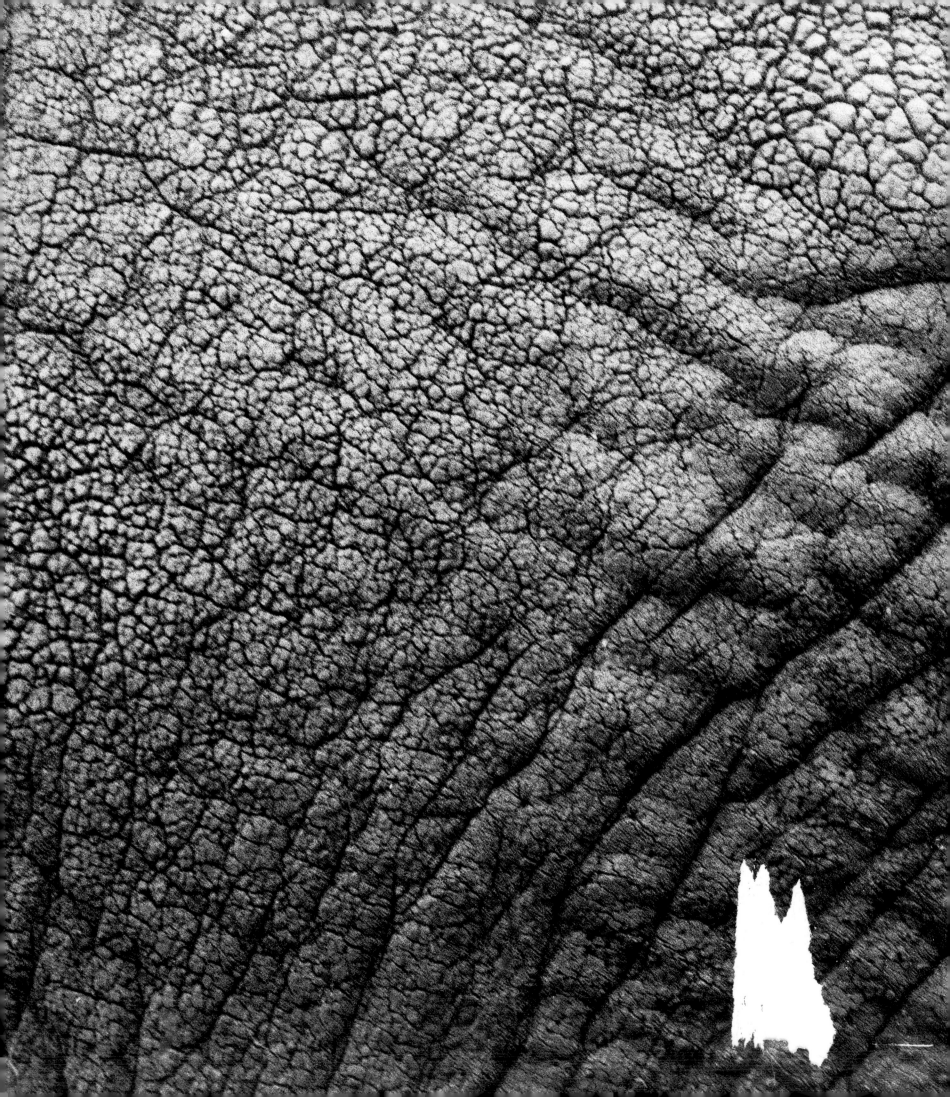